THE
HURT/HELP
BOOK

THE HURT/HELP BOOK

The Ultimate Guide on How To Recognize, Eliminate, and Prevent Troubled Behavior

Tavackus Dawson

Copyright © 2017 Tavackus Dawson
11 rights reserved.

ISBN: 0998457604
ISBN 13: 9780998457604
Library of Congress Control Number: 2017900768
Los Angeles, CA

I want to first dedicate this book to the Most High for giving me insight to write this literature and for *helping* me when I needed it the most. With your love, grace, and mercy, I am here to pass this knowledge forward through you. I am truly blessed. Thank you.

I also dedicate this book to everyone who has ever had problems with alcohol and/or drug abuse, whether they have overcome the addiction or are still battling with the disease. Bless you.

Lastly, this book is especially dedicated to everyone who has been released from prison, transitioned back into society, and is doing great. It's also for those who are still incarcerated at this very moment or who have relapsed in their recovery or sobriety. I want to let you know that there is always a better option than what we choose for ourselves. With a great support system, some therapeutic rehabilitation, and some self-discipline, you too can and will recover to live a great life again! Bless you as well.

ACKNOWLEDGMENTS

I want to thank all my family, friends, strangers, and anyone in law enforcement who has given me good advice about staying away from drugs and crime. I thank you for not being my enabler. I also want to thank and acknowledge some programs I was part of as a kid: the Just Say No program and D.A.R.E. program. Some of my fondest memories have to be McGruff the Crime Dog coming to our schools, giving speeches, and rewarding us with those shiny sticker badges. Those programs set the foundation for us as kids, whether we chose the right or wrong paths in life. Programs like those planted the seeds in young minds to grow into something extraordinary. *Please*, keep those programs alive and running because they could be a key element in someone's recovery and sobriety in the future. I also want to thank all the rehab programs around the world in assisting others back to a normal state of mind. Lastly, I want to give a big thank-you and shout-out to my RDAP mama, Mrs. Powell; the RDAP program team in Talladega, Alabama; and the After Care program for giving me the proper and necessary tools for my recovery. Keep up the good work, y'all!

CONTENTS

INTRODUCTION

You must be asking yourself what this book is all about. It's all about you, you, you, and more you. It's about how you can bring forth self-help and receive more *help* from others. It's about admitting you have a problem with the way you think and finding a solution to rectify it. It will show you how to detect criminal and troubled behavior in adolescents and adults and give insight into the way they think. It will explain how your mistakes in life and your alarming way of thinking have and will continue to *hurt* you if you allow them to. The book will also explain how you can correct your way of thinking as well as how to *help* yourself.

Trouble is mainly a learned behavior; do you agree? If you agree, then you must agree that with proper counseling or rehab, you can maintain a fulfilling life once you receive that *help*. We've all made mistakes, but what matters the most is that we learn from them and correct them. Well, that's what I hope to help you achieve with the Hurt/Help concept, which has proven to be very effective in one's recovery. All you will need in order to succeed is some *self-determination*. If you are willing to be open-minded and willing to follow your own realistic answers that you will provide in this workbook, I have no doubt you will create a positive outcome by achieving victory over a dismissive way of thinking. I would like you to consider this workbook as a life journal to *help* you stay focused on your journey. The illustrations in the book are merely a reminder of the troubled characteristics and traits we face daily in our lives.

This book contains fourteen characters, and although you might self-identify with more than one, remember that you should not be worried about numbers. Your goal is to REP (*Recognize-Eliminate-Prevent*) the character traits from returning to your life. Remember, it's better to prevent a problem than to cure it.

If you are incarcerated, please take full advantage of all the *free* programs and trades that your facility offers. Self-accomplishments in prison and rehab have proven to be very rewarding once you are released back into society. Remember, recovery starts with *you, you, you,* and more *you*. Prison can *hurt* or *help* you in the way you think; it's all about how you perceive it. I decided to let those unfortunate circumstances *help* me. Yes, that's right; I was once where you are, so I speak from experience and concern. I came up with the Hurt/Help concept and REP method as a tool to keep myself away from negative situations so I could live a healthy lifestyle. Don't look at jail as so much of a bad thing; look at it as being time to get yourself together so you can be more productive in your life and family life once you are released. Using this workbook, if you allow these simple exercises to guide you, you can achieve much success in your recovery and your life. And remember: there's always somebody willing and ready to lend a *helping* hand.

REP

Recognize: to identify with something from having encountered it before, perhaps through someone else

Eliminate: to exclude and completely remove from existence

Prevent: to stop something from arising, existing, or occurring

While it's easy to focus on the reprehensible nature of corrupt behavior, we often ignore the hurt behind it. The REP method gets at that and more. It's to *help* you

- identify the cause of problematic behavior
- understand the ramifications of that behavior
- stop and overcome such behavior permanently, and
- begin to make life-affirming choices to become your best self

CHAPTER 1

DRUG DEALER

SYNDROME:

- If I don't sell it to them, somebody else will.
- I'm not forcing anybody to buy it; it's their choice!
- They shouldn't be doing it if they can't handle it!
- I didn't make them lose their family!
- I have to make this big money so my family can have a better life!

Note: A drug dealer is someone who has no boundaries regarding whom he or she sells illegal narcotics to. This individual does not consider selling drugs an addiction; on the contrary, the addiction is greed for money or anything of value.

To the best of your knowledge, give examples and explain how _hurt_ has been a part of the drug dealer's life.

HURT

_____

_____

_____

_____

_____

_____

_____

_____

_____

_____

_____

Now explain what can be done to *help* the drug dealer's irrational thinking.

HELP

_____

_____

_____

_____

_____

_____

_____

_____

_____

_____

_____

Explain what you see in the illustration.

_____

_____

_____

_____

_____

_____

_____

_____

_____

_____

_____

_____

_____

_____

What is your definition of a drug dealer?

_____

_____

_____

_____

_____

_____

_____

_____

_____

_____

_____

_____

_____

_____

Draw a detailed illustration of what a drug dealer looks like to you.

CHAPTER 2

DRUG USER

SYNDROME:

- I get high, but not all the time like I did before.
- I'm not hurting anyone; I'm just having a little fun.
- I've been doing this for years; I'm a pro at it.
- I do it to relax; I'm not addicted to it like that.
- I can quit anytime I want.

Note: A drug user is someone who consumes a drug by smoking, injecting, snorting, or swallowing it. Drug users hurt themselves and those who love them. They will often manipulate whomever they can to get their drugs.

To the best of your knowledge, give examples and explain how the *hurt* has been a part of the drug user's life.

HURT

_____

_____

_____

_____

_____

_____

_____

_____

_____

_____

_____

Now explain what can be done to _help_ the drug user's life.

HELP

_____

_____

_____

_____

_____

_____

_____

_____

_____

_____

_____

Explain what you see in the illustration.

_____

_____

_____

_____

_____

_____

_____

_____

_____

_____

_____

_____

_____

_____

What is your definition of a drug user?

Draw a detailed illustration of what a drug user looks like to you.

CHAPTER 3

ENABLER

SYNDROME:

- I understand exactly what you're going through; life isn't fair.
- That's right, baby; take care of your family by any means necessary!
- Don't worry; I will take care of it for you.
- If you're going to smoke, smoke in the house; I don't want the neighbors in my business.
- I'm going to pay it off for you this time, but no more after this.

Note: An enabler, also known as a codependent, is a person who is in denial about someone they may know that has a personal problem, and who's willing to overlook the problem out of fear of losing that person- or who's out for one's own personal gain.

To the best of your knowledge, give examples of how the _hurt_ has been a part of an enabler's life.

HURT

_____

_____

_____

_____

_____

_____

_____

_____

_____

_____

_____

Now explain what an enabler can do and say to _help_ someone.

HELP

_____

_____

_____

_____

_____

_____

_____

_____

_____

_____

_____

Explain what you see in the illustration.

_____

_____

_____

_____

_____

_____

_____

_____

_____

_____

_____

_____

_____

What is your definition of an enabler?

_____

_____

_____

_____

_____

_____

_____

_____

_____

_____

_____

_____

_____

_____

Draw a detail illustration of what an enabler looks like to you.

CHAPTER 4

GUILTY BY ASSOCIATION

SYNDROME:

- I was there, but I didn't pull the trigger.
- I gave her the knife, but I didn't tell her to stab them.
- Hello, He said bring the dope to his shop.
- I didn't steal the car; I was just riding with them.
- Just be the lookout person. You don't have to do anything else.

Note: In the eyes of the law, you are as guilty as the person who committed the crime. You are judged by the company you keep and guilty of associating with wrongdoers.

To the best of your knowledge, give examples and explain how you've been _hurt_ by this guiltiness.

HURT

_____

_____

_____

_____

_____

_____

_____

_____

_____

_____

_____

Now explain how you can *help* yourself avoid being guilty by association.

HELP

_____

_____

_____

_____

_____

_____

_____

_____

_____

_____

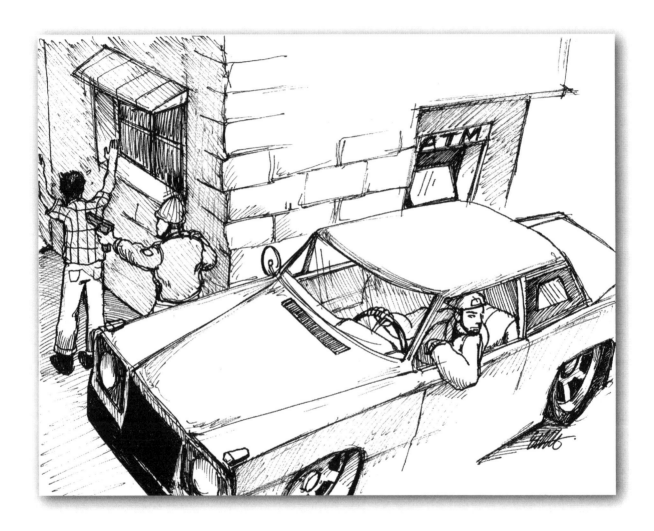

Explain what you see in the illustration.

_____

_____

_____

_____

_____

_____

_____

_____

_____

_____

_____

_____

_____

_____

_____

What is your definition of guilty by association?

_____

_____

_____

_____

_____

_____

_____

_____

_____

_____

_____

_____

_____

Draw a detailed illustration of what guilty by association looks like to you.

CHAPTER 5

WHITE COLLAR CRIMINAL

SYNDROME:

- The money is insured; it can be replaced.
- I can bill them twice for the same service, and they will never notice it.
- I'm making this company millions of dollars; it won't miss a few thousand.
- If these investors don't know what to do with their own money, they shouldn't have it!
- I went shopping with the company credit card; I needed to pay some bills of mine.

Note: Someone who embezzles funds from corporations commits identity theft or fraud. The victims of these crimes are highly traumatized, and they suffer great depression after these horrific events have been committed. The effect of these crimes is that the victims often succumb to death due to stress or suicide.

To the best of your knowledge, give examples and explain how this person has _hurt_ the victim.

Hurt

_____

_____

_____

_____

_____

_____

_____

_____

_____

_____

_____

Now explain how this person can use _help_ to avoid these actions in the future.

HELP

_____

_____

_____

_____

_____

_____

_____

_____

_____

_____

Explain what you see in the illustration.

_____

_____

_____

_____

_____

_____

_____

_____

_____

_____

_____

_____

_____

What is your definition of a white collar criminal?

Draw a detailed illustration of what a white-collar criminal looks like to you.

CHAPTER 6

SENSE OF ENTITLEMENT

SYNDROME:

- I shouldn't have to work!
- They don't deserve that!
- Do you know who I am?
- My family is rich!
- You owe me this!

Note: A sense of entitlement is most commonly found in people who are selfish and egoistical. Their pride clouds their better judgment regarding how they should treat people.

To the best of your knowledge, explain how a sense of entitlement has _hurt_ you.

HURT

Now explain how you can *help* control your sense of entitlement.

HELP

_____

_____

_____

_____

_____

_____

_____

_____

_____

_____

_____

Explain what you see in the illustration.

_____

_____

_____

_____

_____

_____

_____

_____

_____

_____

_____

_____

_____

_____

What is your definition of a sense of entitlement?

Draw a detailed illustration of what a sense of entitlement looks like to you.

CHAPTER 7

ABUSER

SYNDROME:

- You will never amount to anything!
- I'm the man of this house, dammit!
- They are my kids, and I will discipline them however I want!
- He's my husband, so he's my property!
- You made me hit you; I'm sorry.

Note: Abuse is described as being negative toward someone emotionally, physically, sexually, and/or most commonly verbally. An abuser acts with a distraught mind.

To the best of your knowledge, give examples and explain how you *hurt* someone by being an abuser.

HURT

_____

_____

_____

_____

_____

_____

_____

_____

_____

_____

_____

_____

Now explain what this person can do to _help_ him- or herself from being an abuser.

HELP

_____

_____

_____

_____

_____

_____

_____

_____

_____

_____

Explain what you see in the illustration.

_____

_____

_____

_____

_____

_____

_____

_____

_____

_____

_____

_____

_____

_____

_____

What is your definition of an abuser?

Draw a detailed illustration of what an abuser looks like to you.

CHAPTER 8

BULLY

SYNDROME:

- Because I said so!
- No, because you are gay!
- Don't speak to them; they don't believe as we do.
- I'm the boss; your job is at stake if you don't.
- Do it, or get beat up!

Note: A bully is someone who uses power, strength, and/or manipulation to harm others. Bullies can come from family, friends, strangers, and coworkers. Kids can mimic the bullying trait and demonstrate it at school.

To the best of your knowledge, give examples and explain how you _hurt_ someone by being a bully.

HURT

_____

_____

_____

_____

_____

_____

_____

_____

_____

_____

_____

Now explain what can be done to *help* a bully eliminate his or her bullying trait.

HELP

_____

_____

_____

_____

_____

_____

_____

_____

_____

_____

_____

Explain what you see in the illustration.

_____

_____

_____

_____

_____

_____

_____

_____

_____

_____

_____

_____

_____

_____

What is your definition of a bully?

Draw a detailed illustration of what a bully looks like to you.

CHAPTER 9

PROSTITUTE

SYNDROME:

- I'm a single parent; I need to feed my family!
- I have to use what I have to get what I want.
- I was violated when I was younger; no one cares about me!
- I'm not hurting anyone; it's my body!
- I can't make it off paychecks alone; times are hard.

Note: A prostitute is someone who solicits him- or herself sexually for a payment. Prostitutes come in all ages, both male and female, and the experience is not always consensual.

To the best of your knowledge, give examples and explain how prostitution _hurts_ someone.

Hurt

_____

_____

_____

_____

_____

_____

_____

_____

_____

_____

_____

Now explain what can be done to _help_ eliminate prostitution.

HELP

Explain what you see in the illustration.

_____

_____

_____

_____

_____

_____

_____

_____

_____

_____

_____

_____

_____

PROSTITUTE

What is your definition of a prostitute?

Draw a detailed illustration of what prostitution looks like to you.

CHAPTER 10

GAMBLER

SYNDROME:

- I feel as if I'm about to hit it big!
- No, I'm not leaving; I must win this money!
- I can't lose; I'm on a winning streak!
- I'm a pro at this; I have it down to a science.
- Loan me some money; I will pay you back double!

Note: A gambler is someone who sets a wager or risks money, property, or anything of value for a chance of winning. There are many levels to gambling, which often lead to illegal activities. When gamblers lose, irrational thinking tells them all they need is more money to win.

To the best of your knowledge, give examples and explain how gambling has _hurt_ you or someone you know.

HURT

_____

_____

_____

_____

_____

_____

_____

_____

_____

_____

_____

_____

Now explain what can be done to _help_ a gambler eliminate this addiction.

HELP

_____

_____

_____

_____

_____

_____

_____

_____

_____

_____

_____

Explain what you see in the illustration.

_____

_____

_____

_____

_____

_____

_____

_____

_____

_____

_____

_____

_____

_____

_____

What is your definition of a gambler?

Draw a detailed illustration of what a gambler looks like to you.

CHAPTER 11

CONVICT

SYNDROME:

- I shouldn't be here!
- This isn't fair!
- Screw the law!
- The judge and the prosecutor had it out for me!
- This is my last time going to jail!

Note: A convict is someone who has been found guilty of a crime, and he or she then serves a prison sentence. Most convicts feel everyone is out to see them fail, when actually they are their own worst enemies. Knowing better means doing better.

To the best of your knowledge, give examples and explain how becoming a convict has _hurt_ you or someone else.

HURT

_____

_____

_____

_____

_____

_____

_____

_____

_____

_____

Now explain what can be done to _help_ a convict eliminate irrational thinking.

HELP

_____

_____

_____

_____

_____

_____

_____

_____

_____

_____

_____

_____

Explain what you see in the illustration.

_____

_____

_____

_____

_____

_____

_____

_____

_____

_____

_____

_____

_____

_____

What is your definition of a convict?

_____

_____

_____

_____

_____

_____

_____

_____

_____

_____

_____

_____

_____

_____

Draw a detailed illustration of what a convict looks like to you.

CHAPTER 12

GANGSTER

SYNDROME:

- The world belongs to me!
- I'm unstoppable, and I do what I want!
- I will achieve it by any means necessary!
- I'm above the law!
- I would rather they fear me than love me!

Note: A gangster is a member of a violent criminal organization. Gangsters have a great sense of entitlement and feel the law is beneath them. They will go to great lengths to illegally achieve what they desire, even if it means using lethal force.

To the best of your knowledge, give examples and explain how a gangster has _hurt_ society.

HURT

_____

_____

_____

_____

_____

_____

_____

_____

_____

_____

_____

_____

_____

Now explain what can be done to _help_ a gangster rectify his or her way of living.

HELP

Explain what you see in the illustration.

_____

_____

_____

_____

_____

_____

_____

_____

_____

_____

_____

_____

_____

What is your definition of a gangster and his/ or her lifestyle?

Draw a detailed illustration of what a gangster looks like to you.

CHAPTER 13

NEEDING ANGER MANAGEMENT

SYNDROME:

- I don't need a crazy shrink messing with my head!
- If people would just mind their own freaking business…
- I'm not your child; don't tell me what to do!
- No one helps me do anything; I'm all alone in this world!
- I hate you; I wish you would just die!

Note: Anger management is for someone who needs *help* dealing with his or her anger. You must first admit you have anger issues to manage it. We all experience anger frequently due to frustration. Anger management teaches you how to properly deploy your anger successfully.

To the best of your knowledge, give examples and explain how you've allowed anger to *hurt* yourself or someone else.

HURT

_____

_____

_____

_____

_____

_____

_____

_____

_____

_____

_____

Now explain what could be the benefits of receiving _help_ from anger-management programs.

HELP

Explain what you see in the illustration.

_____

_____

_____

_____

_____

_____

_____

_____

_____

_____

_____

_____

_____

_____

_____

What is your definition of anger?

Draw a detailed illustration of what anger looks like to you.

CHAPTER 14

MANIPULATOR

SYNDROME:

- If it were me, I would do it for you.
- If you truly loved me, you would buy it.
- I knew you were too scared. I'll do it myself!
- Just this one time. I promise I won't ask again.
- If it were me, I wouldn't take it.

Note: A manipulator is someone who consistently attempts to use his or her dishonest behavior for personal benefit. Manipulators often participate in wrongdoing to gain your trust. They tend to play the victim role for sympathy.

To the best of your knowledge, give examples and explain how you _hurt_ someone by being the manipulator.

HURT

_____

_____

_____

_____

_____

_____

_____

_____

_____

_____

Now explain what can be done to _help_ a manipulator eliminate this way of thinking.

Help

_____

_____

_____

_____

_____

_____

_____

_____

_____

_____

Explain what you see in the illustration.

What is your definition of a manipulator?

Draw a detailed illustration of what a manipulator looks like to you.

What character(s) could you relate to the most? Explain how and why.

TEST YOUR KNOWLEDGE AND MATCH

You are so stupid!	Drug user
Give me your lunch money!	Gambler
Who cares what you think!	Manipulator
You misunderstood me.	Abuser
I'm on a roll tonight!	White-collar criminal
It's easy money!	Sense of entitlement
I smoke a few days of the week.	Anger management
We're getting real money!	Bully
They are good boys.	Drug dealer
Lucky me. Someone's credit card.	Prostitute
I hate you!	Enabler

GLOSSARY

Achieve: to bring about or reach something successfully; by effort, skill, or courage.

Ambition: a strong desire to do or to achieve something typically requiring determination and hard work.

Behavior: the way in which one acts or conducts oneself, especially towards other people.

Counseling: the provision of assistance and guidance in resolving personal, social, or psychological problems and difficulties, especially by a professional.

Dismissive: feeling or showing that something is unworthy of consideration.
Faith: to believe it was meant to happen for you.

Help: being able to receive beneficial assistance from someone.

Hurt: inflicting physical or emotional pain or injury to yourself or someone else.

Method: a particular form of procedure for accomplishing or approaching something systematically or established.

Motivation: the willingness and desire to accomplish something.

Obstacles: a thing that blocks one's way or prevents or hinders progress.

Open-minded: willing to consider ideas and opinions that are new or different to your own; change.

Patience: capability to accept or tolerate delay without getting upset.

Positive: with no possibility of doubt; a good, affirmative, or constructive quality or attribute.

Prepare: to make (someone or something) ready for some activity, purpose, or something you will be doing or that you expect to happen.

Self-determination: the process by which a person controls his or her own life.

Self-discipline: the ability to control one's feelings and overcome one's weakness; the ability to pursue what one thinks is right despite temptations to abandon it.

Self-worth: the sense of one's own value or worth as a person; self-esteem; self-respect.

Strategy: a plan of action or policy designed to achieve a major or overall aim; masterplan.

Success: the accomplishment of an aim, purpose, or prosperity.

Trouble: To cause problems, difficulty, distress, or disorder.

RESOURCES

Alcoholics Anonymous: (AA) www.aa.org

Cocaine Anonymous: (CA) www.ca.org

Domestic violence: www.thehotline.org

Families Anonymous: www.familiesanonymous.org

Gamblers Anonymous: www.gambleranonymous.org

Intervention Workshop: www.interventionworkshop.com

Marijuana Anonymous: www.marijuana-anonymous.org

Narcotics Anonymous: www.na.org

National Anger Management Association: (NAMA) www.namass.org

National hotline phone numbers: www.recovery-worldhotline.com (This hotline will provide *help* for any recovery you need.)

National Institute on Drug Abuse: www.drugabuse.gov

Prostitution Recovery: www.prostitutionrecovery.org

Stop Bullying: www.stopbullying.gov

FINAL THOUGHTS

We've all heard that song "Man in The Mirror" by the late, great singer Michael Jackson. Well, that's what this book is about in many ways. The reasons for writing this book were merely to *help* enlighten, motivate, and give insight into how to successfully achieve self-help. This book passes no judgment in any way, shape, or form. This book also does not discriminate toward color, race, creed, religion, or sex. No one can tell you how to deal with your pain or how to grieve over something tragic that has happened to you, but keeping those feelings suppressed won't make it any better either. We all need *help* from someone once in our lives. The world we live in isn't perfect, so it's OK when you feel as if it has let you down. But don't let it stop you from becoming who you should be. If you have fallen in your recovery or sobriety, pick yourself up, and try again. The world is rooting for you; I'm rooting for you! The ol' saying goes, "It takes a village to raise a child." Well, I'm a part of that worldwide village, and I'm doing my part by writing and sharing this knowledge so all communities can benefit from it. I pray and hope that everyone can have as much success with the Hurt/Help theory as I have. I feel that if I can positively touch one soul with this book, I will have done one of my God-given duties in this world. May we all have a blessed life.

HAPPY LIST

My name is:_____

I'm _____ years old.

My goals are:_____

I'm happy when:_____

I love:_____

My biggest accomplishment:_____

I would love to travel to_____ and do_____

My fondest memories are:_____

I like to imagine:_____

I'm inspired by:_____

I help others :_____

My favorite food and restaurant is:_____

My favorite music, and instrument is:_____

My favorite book and art is:_____

My favorite T.V. show is:_____

My favorite play is:_____

I love to shop at:_____ and_____

I love to be outdoors in nature:_____

INSPIRATIONAL QUOTES

T. DAWSON, entrepreneur, author, motivational speaker: "They say it's a cold world we live in, I say dress warmer to weather the storm."

DENZEL WASHINGTON, actor, director, and producer: "You got to do what you got to do in order to do what you want to do."

MALIK YOBA, actor, writer, and singer: "Build your own generator so when they turn off the power, you can still have lights."

TYLER PERRY, actor, songwriter, director, and author: "Plant your seed, water it, and believe."

STEVE HARVEY, comedian, actor, and radio personality: "God is in the blessing business."

SMOKIE NORFUL, singer, pianist: "I Need You Now."

BRIAN GOODALL JR., songwriter and producer: "You will never know where you should be until you know who you are."

BETSY WEIGLE, entrepreneur and teacher: "The only path from a broken lifestyle to a healthy one is knowledge."

MIGUEL DE CERVANTES, writer and novelist: "The man who is prepared has his battle half fought."

Entrepreneur Magazine: "When you can't get a job, create a job."

PUBLISHER'S NOTE

ARE YOU LOOKING TO CHANGE YOUR WAY OF THINKING TO A POSITIVE ONE? IF SO, THIS BOOK IS FOR YOU.

In life, we have choices, and how we make those choices will determine the outcome in our lives. Throughout the year, we wear many head garments for the different seasons due to weather changing. Well using your "Thinking Cap" serves as a much greater headwear also.

Before leaving a doctor's visit; with proper diagnosis; they prescribe medication, advise a strict diet to follow if needed, and most important exercise right. That's because exercising is a key component to maintaining a healthy life, and exercising your brain with the proper material is no different. The exercises in this workbook will HELP you do just that, in achieving your positive thinking.

Remember your goal in life should be, to be, the best you can be, that you were meant to be. If you would learn to REP, (Recognize, Eliminate, and Prevent) your problem, as is occurs; you will be able to control how far it develops. I present to you,

"THE HURT/HELP BOOK"

[The Author] like anyone else, has had his share of run ins with troubled behavior. He has overcome a lot of obstacles he created in life, through trial and error. He speaks from years of experience with the knowledge he shares in this book. He hates being told he's an exception to the rule, as to why he *made it*. Dawson believes everyone can *make it* or achieve success through self-determination. A native from Louisiana via Los Angeles; he's an active pillar in the community where he speaks and motivates others to become a better them. BOOKING INFO. Tavackus@yahoo.com

Notes

Comments   **Page No.**

Notes

Comments   Page No.

Made in the USA
Lexington, KY
30 March 2017